CHURCHIN' AIN'T EASY

WHAT ALL CHRISTIANS NEED TO KNOW BUT FEW TAKE THE TIME TO SHARE!

JENNIFER GILBERT

iUniverse, Inc.
Bloomington

Churchin' Ain't Easy
What All Christians Need to Know But Few Take the Time to Share!

iUniverse books may be ordered through booksellers or by contacting:

iUniverse
1663 Liberty Drive
Bloomington, IN 47403
www.iuniverse.com
1-800-Authors (1-800-288-4677)

Because of the dynamic nature of the Internet, any web addresses or links contained in this book may have changed since publication and may no longer be valid. The views expressed in this work are solely those of the author and do not necessarily reflect the views of the publisher, and the publisher hereby disclaims any responsibility for them.

Any people depicted in stock imagery provided by Thinkstock are models, and such images are being used for illustrative purposes only.

Certain stock imagery © Thinkstock.

ISBN: 978-1-4502-9089-0 (sc)
ISBN: 978-1-4502-9091-3 (dj)
ISBN: 978-1-4502-9090-6 (ebook)

Printed in the United States of America

iUniverse rev. date: 02/14/2011

To the Almighty God, thank you for your grace and mercy in my life!

Damaria and J'Donte Henderson, thanks for all the sacrifice of mommy-time that you endured so I could do all that God has called me to do. I love you so much!

To all my friends and family who have supported and encouraged me in my efforts, thanks, and to those who didn't, I sincerely thank you more!

To the bestest friend in the whole world, Sherronda Randle, thanks for just letting me be me. When I'm silly, sad, frustrated, or mad, thanks for loving me in spite of it.

To my father, Lester Adams, thanks for letting me know that I am always going to be daddy's baby girl. I know that our latter will be greater than our past.

To my big brother, Charles Adams, thanks for being the man of my life for the longest time as well as my children's lives. I have always looked up to you so I hope this makes you and mama proud. I love you so much but I refuse to stay single forever … lol.

There is power in perseverance through painful persecution.

—*Jennifer Gilbert*

CONTENTS

FOREWORD

There comes a time in life when everyone has an experience that speaks directly to a specific situation in his or her life. That experience will be life-changing and actually manifest a truth or revelation that will clear questions and frustrations that have kept your spirit bound for years. This book is the experience that I would recommend to all Christians, young, old, inexperienced, and experienced. Minister Jennifer Gilbert has allowed the Holy Spirit to really simple and yet powerful truth of releasing the saints of God from church bondage. This book is so simple to read, yet it holds so many truths concerning the *real church*. In this book, Minister Gilbert speaks to all people in all churches, in all church denominations and in all races. She clears up the dogma in church politics, speaks of Christ's preference of relationships over religion, and simply explains why *Churchin' Ain't Easy*.

This book gives the people of God a basic outline of the misconception and untruth that has bound Christians for years. Minister Gilbert outlines and documents the what, why, where, and how of why churchin' ain't easy. One of my favorite chapters is "Why So Many?" Her answer for why there are so many churches is worth more than the price of the book. Another favorite chapter is "What Am I Supposed to Do Now?" This chapter speaks to all people who seem to be in between life's destruction and life's destiny. So you made it into the church, gave your life to Christ, are on the worship and praise team, but you're still dealing with devils. You may be wondering if you should get off the praise team until you're fully delivered. Should you feel guilty because you still have a specific problem? For years, you have dealt with *your* besetting sin but to no avail. Yes, saints. *Churchin' Ain't Easy.* My advice is for you to read this book. It will give you a clear, concise, and godly counsel on how to look at yourself through the eyes of God—biblically and righteously.

I was blessed to have had the opportunity to be Minister Jennifer Gilbert's pastor for a season, and I can attest to the fact that she is an anointed vessel, used of God in the prophetic and in worship and now as an author. *Churchin' Ain't Easy* is a must-read for newcomers in Christ. It will eliminate so much confusion for new converts as to their places in the church and their relationships with Christ. As for seasoned saints, we need this book to help us recalibrate our navigational systems. Most of us are using the right tools, but our tools have not been calibrated for years.

Apostle Cartrell Woods
Dominion Life Fellowship
Killeen, Texas

PREFACE

They've prayed forever that you would be saved. In every conversation with friends and family, they have always alluded to the fact that if you had the Lord in your life, things would be different for you. So now you have gotten the revelation and given your life to Christ—so now what? It's a place of transition, not to mention the discomfort of the new expectations that sometimes seem overwhelming. You can no longer talk to your unsaved friends because they somehow feel betrayed by you or often state that you have changed. You can't talk to all the church people because they make you feel uncomfortable. This book is designed to help you through your transitional experience.

This book is for all individuals who have recently given their lives to Christ and find themselves experiencing a valley experience, not knowing which way to go. Your worldly friends seem to think that you have changed too much, and the church folks say that you haven't changed enough, so you find yourself lonely and confused, wondering if you made the right choice. Well, I am here to tell you that yes, you did—and where to go from here. When the excitement and the zeal that you had when you first came to Christ have been tainted by the judgments and expectations of man, how do you keep the balance of being of service to the earth and to heaven? It's not easy, but it can be done.

I have been in church for over thirty years, and I was raised in the United States and abroad, thanks to the military. I have even been a part of various denominations and have seen the differences in the expectations and the words that are spoken, which brought me to the conclusion that my relationship with Christ is just that: a relationship, not a religion. Had someone explained that to me when I first converted, that revelation would have saved me a lot of heartache, headaches, tears, and sorrow. Now that I have that revelation, I see that there is hope for tomorrow, and the reality is that *Churchin' Ain't Easy!*

ABOUT THE AUTHOR

 Jennifer Gilbert is a well-known preacher, teacher, prophet, and praise-and-worship leader throughout Texas and the surrounding areas. Born in Lawton, Oklahoma, but raised worldwide by a military family while overcoming very serious and personal issues, she answered her call to God at the tender age of nine, but due to oppression of others' opinions, she did not fully walk in her calling until 2002. She is an honored high school graduate of Bradwell Institute in Hinesville, Georgia, class of 1993. She completed the beginning of her college career with a high-honored associate's degree in child development as well as business administration and has completed her bachelor's in the same areas of expertise at Tarleton State University. She completed her master's in education at the University of Phoenix and is currently pursuing a double doctorate—one in educational leadership from the University of Phoenix and the other from Northwestern Theological Seminary in Christian education.

Jennifer has served faithfully in many positions, both past and present. Some of those positions have included head of pastors' support, lead intercessor, youth pastor, head of youth drama ministry, head of youth mime ministry, choir member and assistant choir director, president of the YPD (Young People's Division), praise-and-worship leader, overseer of the financial committee, outreach ministry, evangelism, and administration. Her greatest loves, second to God, are her two children, Damaria and J'Donte (J. J.) Henderson, who reside with her in Killeen, Texas.

Her famous quote is "There is power in perseverance through painful persecution." She coined this quote during the painful persevering pursuit of her deliverance from years of abusive relationships and other strongholds that were overcome by the grace of God and radical perseverance against all odds. This means that the more that you persevere in the face of painful persecution, be it from yourself or others, the more powerful you become.

She believes that her ultimate gift is to teach, preach, and share a tangible Jesus—one whose heart can be touched through authentic praise and worship, individually and corporately, through honest *relationship, not religion.*

ACKNOWLEDGMENTS

First and foremost, to God for his grace and mercy to see me through my life and this project. To my first pastor extraordinaire, Pastor A. W. Colbert, for always trying to keep me on the straight and narrow and being in my business even when not invited. I would like to acknowledge all the individuals as well as churches that have helped me in my walk along the way. No matter where I go or what I do, you will always be my first true pastor. To all the other pastors and laypersons who have touched my life at different times, there are too many to name, but your names are all over this book as well. Thanks for the investment.

To Apostle Cartrell Woods, thanks for a wonderful foreword and just to you and first lady (Prophetess Nedith Woods) for being my mom and dad in the faith. I have watched you all endure many storms and, like God, I have seen your posture and I have been blessed by your perseverance. Keep on moving and know that I will always be there.

To June Cornish, my auntie, and another spiritual mother … Man, you have invested so much in my life. You filled in so many blanks about my past so that I can walk into my destiny as a whole woman of God instead of the fragmented pieces that I once was. I know my mom appreciates you helping me to see her in a different light after her death and allowing healing to take place. Though we don't talk nearly as often as I'd like, I do thank God for the words that you do impart unto me.

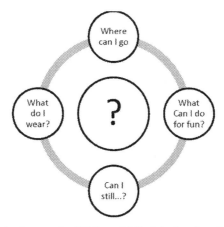

You don't have to change who YOU are, let God do the changing in HIS time!

CHAPTER ONE
WELCOME

Now that you have joined the body of Christ, let me first take the time to welcome you to the family of God.

Christian change takes place from the inside out. This means that the first works start with your heart and then transcend to the outer person, wherein it is made evident of the presence of God in your life. You will find many scriptures in the Bible that talk about matters of the heart. Oftentimes we are put into a box when we come into the body of Christ, and we are overwhelmed with the changes and expectations of the church. We are told that we can't dress this way, we can't drink this, we can't eat this, and we have to act this way. Not so! Please understand that none of us were born saved and speaking in tongues, and though some have been saved so long that they forgot their original struggle, you are not alone. We have all have our crosses to bear, and if the truth be told, we are still struggling with some of our original issues as well.

We have just learned the church lingo and mannerisms enough to mask or camouflage our shortcomings.

As a child raised around the military for the majority of my life, I have seen all types of soldiers and their various personalities and perceptions. When we, as civilians, look at them when they are in uniform, we see them all as soldiers, but we never get to know all of them as individuals and learn about the various struggles that they go through. Looking from the outside in, they all seem the same and represent the same thing, but at the end of the day, they all have different backgrounds and upbringings, and they all have different visions and goals in mind. When you talk to them and ask them why they decided to join the armed forces, some of them will say they did it to escape where they were from, some did it to pay off student loans, and some did it to overcome the obstacles of the economical issues of our world. So it is with the body of Christ. Many people gave their lives to Christ for the benefits but never thought of the suffering that comes with the territory.

When you welcome Christ into your heart, you subliminally welcome the scrutiny of individuals. These individuals can be close to you or may even be you yourself. We are often our worst enemies and biggest critics. As you welcome Christ into your heart, be sure to welcome the freedom and new life that comes with this act. No matter how you feel or what you go through, always know that there is a level of suffering, but with perseverance, there is a level of glory as well that you have yet to tap into. Take these words of encouragement as well as warning as you proceed through this book. Know that we all have days when we feel super-saved, as though we can save the world, and then on the flip side, there are also those days when we feel as though we can't take another step! *You can!*

> *For I reckon that the sufferings of this present time are not worthy to be compared with the glory which shall be revealed in us.*
>
> —*Romans 8:18 (KJV)*

Do not be deceived; God is not mocked! That means we can fool man, but we cannot fool God. God knows all your intentions and reasoning for giving your life to him. He even knows the very motive of the day that you made the choice. He knows if you were caught up in the moment or if it was a cry of desperation that came from a pure heart with good intentions. Through this book, my prayer is to show you how to tackle some of the biggest issues that you may encounter when either searching for a church home or being newly placed in the one that you accepted Christ in. Hopefully, I can help make the load a little lighter for you and set you up for a successful relationship with Christ in heaven.

CHAPTER ONE: WELCOME

What are some things that I desire for God to change in me?

_____
_____
_____
_____
_____
_____
_____
_____
_____
_____
_____
_____
_____
_____
_____
_____
_____
_____
_____
_____
_____
_____
_____
_____
_____
_____
_____
_____
_____
_____

_____
_____
_____
_____
_____
_____
_____
_____
_____
_____
_____
_____
_____
_____
_____
_____
_____
_____
_____
_____
_____
_____
_____
_____
_____
_____
_____
_____
_____
_____

This list will assist you in recognizing the things that you need to begin incorporating into your daily prayer life—the hidden things that you want God to change in you (e.g., a bad attitude, a quick temper, an addiction, etc.).

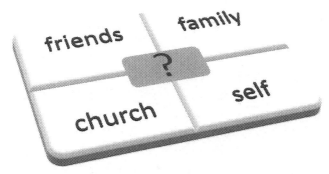

So many expectations from so many people, what do I do?

WHAT AM I SUPPOSED TO DO NOW?

There comes a time in everyone's walk when this question pops up: *What am I supposed to do now?* This question is posed from one end of the spectrum to the other. You may ask yourself what you are supposed to do when the following occurs:

- The church won't accept you and neither will the world.

- They want you to dress a certain way, but you don't have the means or the attire to accommodate the expectation.

- They expect you to pay tithes when you can't afford to feed your children.

- You don't know who to talk to about the situation that you are going through, and no one really seems to understand or care.

- What do you do when the "prophet" is prophesying or prophelying to you and you're standing there at the altar with all eyes on you, while others are looking for a reaction?

So many questions come with the new relationship with Christ. That could be an entirely separate book in itself, and we still wouldn't exhaust all the questions. Some will be answered in one way or another in this book. I would advise you to have a personal relationship with Christ wherein he can and will answer all your questions personally, through the word of God or through a person. Regarding your having a personal relationship with Christ, I am speaking of constantly communing with him through prayer and talking with him. Please know that it is not the use of a bunch of words that moves the heart of God but the heart from which those words are spoken. When you do this, there will be no question as to whether it is correct or authentic because it will resound in your inner being.

When you start a new earthly relationship, you establish that relationship by communicating with that person and spending time getting to know that special someone. When you meet new people, you will learn what turns them on and off, what makes them happy or sad—and you will also learn things about their past, present, and future. So it is with your relationship with Christ. You should have a desire to get to know all about him and begin to recognize all that he has done in the past Bible days as well as how he is currently manifesting himself in your life and how he will do it yet again in the future as you draw closer to him. These are just some of the components that you can begin with when establishing your relationship with Christ.

CHAPTER TWO:
WHAT AM I SUPPOSED TO DO NOW?

What are five questions that I wish someone would answer?

1. _____
   _____
   _____

2. _____
   _____
   _____

3. _____
   _____
   _____

4. _____
   _____
   _____

5. _____
   _____
   _____

These questions are only for the eyes of you and God, and that is from whom you should seek the answers, opening yourself to the avenues that he provides to bring you the answers.

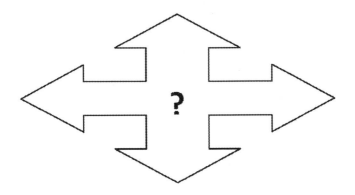

CHAPTER THREE
WHY SO MANY?

In these times, when there are churches on virtually most corners, you have every right to be selective as to the one that you attend. This truly has to be a personal decision; it cannot be based on the opinions of others but your own personal revelation of who you are, who God is in your life, and the calling that you feel God has placed over your life. You have to find a church that suits your spiritual needs, and no one knows those needs but you and God. Many people feel that the church in which they gave their life to Christ has to be their home church. This is not necessarily true.

Consider this analogy given to me by Apostle Cartrell Woods; this was a revelatory word if I have ever received one, and I internalized and adopted it into my own language. Churches can be likened to the education system: there are some schools for Head Start, elementary, middle school or intermediate, and high school, and then there is the collegiate level—but the learning doesn't stop there. It goes on to grad school. Every church has its own purpose and audience (congregation) that it serves. You have to graduate from one level and move on to another level. What we don't want to see is spiritual retardation, wherein you have a collegiate believer in a primary learning setting. This is like putting my son's size ten foot in my size nine women's shoe. It is going to be quite uncomfortable. On the flip side of that same coin, you don't want to have a primary student in a grad school environment wherein he or she cannot understand the language or content that is being conveyed. This is the quickest way to lose members especially if discipleship and Christian training is not available for the undergrad students.

Not only that, but there are different callings within the body of Christ. Certain ministries speak to certain callings more than others do. There are ministries that are called to meet certain needs. If someone wants to learn, then he or she is drawn to ministries that specialize in teaching, churches that may be in the likes of John Hagee's. If one is seeking to develop his or her prophetic ministry, then he or she will have a tendency to be drawn to ministry that specializes in that area and implement the teachings that look deeper than the superficial verbiage that we read in the books but ask, "What does this really mean?" These tendencies would follow teachings such as those by T. D. Jakes and so forth. This is where the impartation and expectation balance comes in. You have to know yourself first in order to understand your beliefs, convictions, callings, and expectations, and then you build on that.

Here are some questions that you need to ask yourself when seeking a church to call home:

1. Do their corporate beliefs echo those that God has given me during my time of personal study?

2. Is the place that I am seeking readily available? Whether it's good music or good preaching, there has to be something there that will hold your interest. (Please remember that it's not all about feelings; you are not on an emotional retreat.) It is all about your calling and your predestined location that God has ordained for you before the foundation of the world. If you can find a church that meets your spiritual need, that is first priority. If there is a great choir or if you make friends, you can view that as an added fringe benefit. But your ultimate goal should be development, discipline, and maturity.

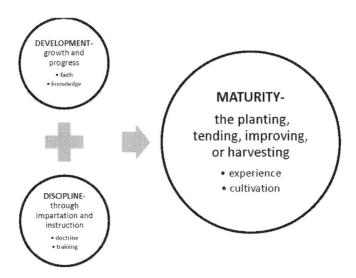

This illustration is designed to show you how to seek balance in your place of worship that is ultimately for the benefit of your relationships both vertically with Christ and horizontally with man. The presence of development and discipline has to be evident in order for the spiritual maturity that you ultimately seek to take place. The discipline is directly correlated to the impartation that needs to take place. The development is correlated to the exploration, and the maturation is made evident in the ability to function to meet the expectations that are present.

When we go on job interviews, not only are the employers interviewing us to see if they want us to work for them, but we should also be interviewing them to see if this is a place in which we can grow and flourish. So it should be in the church. I think that it is wise for believers to interview their pastors prior to committing themselves to the congregation they serve. Here are several things that one should look for when considering a church to join:

- Does the pastor have a vision, and is it clearly posted and understood by him or her and the congregation? The Bible clearly states that without a vision, the people perish. The presence and posting of a vision speaks of life, vitality, and order as well as security. You have to know where you are going as a body to gauge your growth as an individual.

If you cannot see the vision of the body, how can you see where or if you fit in?

- How often are evaluations done in reference to the vision and the synchronization that needs to take place to ensure that the vision is followed? Visions should be revisited on a regular basis. This evaluation allows us to see if we are still on the right track. Have we veered away from the will of God? Have minor matters become major issues that took us off task? These are questions of a wise overseer as well as the members of his congregation.

- How long has the minister been saved? In ministry? In the pastoral position? This is important because you don't want the blind leading the blind. The manner of life of your pastor, as in the way that he or she lives his or her life outside of the pulpit, says a lot about the members that follow his or her lead. How would you be viewed in the community when someone asks you what church you go to and who your pastor is, and as soon as you tell the person, eyes start rolling, blood pressures begin to rise, and comments come pouring out in a negative manner? By the same token, there are always going to be haters at some point, those who don't like them just because, but the general consensus should not be that. It is important for pastors to be real and share their stories so members won't hear them on the street and be shocked and embarrassed.

- How are various elements of life such as singles ministry, couples ministry, teen ministry, outreach, and the like addressed and balanced within the church? Christian life is all about balance, and having ministries such as these allows for the implementation of that balance and also shows that there are acknowledgements to the outside aspects of Christianity. My friend, there is life outside of church and ministries such as the ones listed in this point should teach us how to live that life successfully and how to transition from our worldly thinking to the new frame of mind that we should attain in time after we receive Christ into our hearts.

- Is there a clear and specified order or protocol in the church, and is it truly followed? No matter the size of the church, order is crucial! But order is nothing without implementation and adherence. No wants to be in a place where everyone is a chief and there are no Indians. You also don't want to be in a place where the chiefs are too good or elite to do Indian-type work. I am often amazed at Christian gatherings where the leaders are always seated to be served and never do any of the serving. In order to be a good leader, one must also be a good follower. I, personally, am more apt to take instruction and correction from one who is able to receive it as well; after all, iron sharpens iron. Now don't get me wrong. There is a way to talk to the man and woman of God. There is even a way to ask questions that you may not understand about matters that are going within the church. Remember the mantle to which you are speaking.

- What offerings are there as far as impartation to the life of the healthy Christian? For instance, trainings, Sunday schools, Bible studies, and any developmental ministries. Training is important, especially to new converts, so to go and not grow makes no sense.

- What are the attendance or growth trends for the church body? No one should want to unite with a ministry that has not seen a new member in over thirty days. This is evidence of lack of growth and progress and says a lot about the ministry as a whole.

These are just some of the questions that can be asked before committing yourself to a church body. However, there is a way to ask these questions to ensure that no one is offended. We have to be prayerful in all of our dealings, but a true pastor would appreciate the straightforward approach that this action implies. In addition to asking these questions, you should present your offerings to the ministry as well, just as you would present your résumé to a potential employer. Even if you're not sure what you have to offer, maybe they can assist you in finding out what you can do. While presenting your questions, at least tell them your hobbies, explaining what you do well and allowing them to tell you how your attributes can fit into the vision and the church body.

This conversation does several things for the relationship between you and your potential church:

1. It establishes relationship.

2. It builds rapport.

3. It eliminates any questions.

4. You become more than a new face.

5. It eases the apprehension of attendance.

6. It allows both parties to feel the spirit of the other.

7. It allows the opportunity for prayer and meditation to take place regarding the decisions to be made in reference to the union of the believer and the church.

I remember when I first joined Macedonia Missionary Baptist Church of Galveston, Texas, under the tutelage of Pastor A. W. Colbert. He had what was called the "Pastor's Class" in Sunday school, and it was designed for you to attend this class for maybe six weeks and then graduate and move on to your assigned class. I stayed for at least a year in that class just because I loved his teaching and the way he conducted the class. No, I wasn't alone in this sin; there were a lot of us who did it, so much so that he had to revamp the class and kick us out. That experience allowed me to have a spiritual connection with him both in the natural and in the spiritual sense—he became like a father to me. Because of that connection, when I did something, wrong he knew it. I never had to say a word. He never hesitated to pick up the phone if I was missing from choir rehearsal or anything; he was always there. Keep in mind that I was an adult, but I knew I needed help and so did he, and in a nonintrusive manner, he would step in just in time, before I did something stupid. I respected him for that. In addition, he was well respected in the community and by his wife. That says a lot right there. Sometimes in choir rehearsal, we would have a question about something happening in the church. We would look at Sister Linda Colbert, and she would look back at us and say, "I don't know why ya'll looking at me. I don't know. When it comes to matters of this church, I'm a member, just like ya'll!" We would all laugh because it was true and evident. Not in a bad way. There was just something about Pastor Colbert that was medicine to all our souls. You could tell Pastor something and you never, and I do mean *never*, heard it repeated. These attributes made him such a wonderful pastor to me.

When I first went to that church, I had purposed in my heart that I was only going to get a friend to leave me alone about going to church. I had already been hurt in churches in the past. Specifically, I had sent a note to my old pastor on a Sunday morning and told him that I was going to go home and kill myself. I meant it too, yet I didn't hear from that pastor for two to three weeks after I had unsuccessfully tried. So I went to Macedonia with a friend and was blown away but still rebelling. Finally, about my second or third time going, the word was so piercing that my heart was softened, but I couldn't move past the pain that I was wallowing in, and I remember Pastor Colbert standing there saying to the congregation during the altar call, "I hear your hurt. Who am I talking to? Listen, let me apologize for that pastor who did you wrong! I'm sorry. Just give God another chance! You made it through that for a reason. Let's see why." My heart raced as the tears fell, and instantly I felt light as a feather as I ran to the altar. He came down from the pulpit and held me with his hands. I felt his big heart, and the rest is history. I never shared with him who the other pastor was. It wasn't important, because all things were made new. I was giving God another chance.

Back to the chapter at hand: I was disciplined by his love, developed in my faith, and matured in my walk when I was there. Even though I am far away now, Macedonia will always be my church home.

CHAPTER 3: WHY SO MANY?

Go visit five churches and then compare them as far as what you liked and disliked. Then rank the objectives below from one to five, with one being complete dislike and five being the one liked most.

Preaching	1	2	3	4	5
Teaching	1	2	3	4	5
Singing	1	2	3	4	5
Development	1	2	3	4	5
Discipline	1	2	3	4	5

Extension: *Look at the questions presented in this chapter and take a few to the leaders of the churches you visit. Observe and journal their reactions to help you make your decision.*

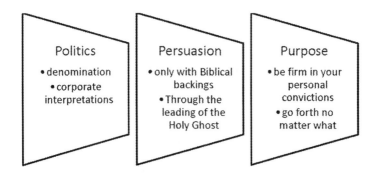

Politics	Persuasion	Purpose
• denomination • corporate interpretations	• only with Biblical backings • Through the leading of the Holy Ghost	• be firm in your personal convictions • go forth no matter what

POLITICS, PERSUASION, AND PURPOSE

POLITICS

If we are going to partake in the church experience, then we need to understand some fundamental truths of Christendom that few people take time to understand or even research. The main thing is that a governmental structure that is present in the church ensures that all things are done decently and in order. Everyone's interpretation of this truth varies, which is where the various denominations come from. Without getting too historical about the matter, denominations came about because someone thought that he or she had a better revelation of how to do things or how to govern the matters of the church. The bottom line is that there were always those in the church, be it right or wrong, who stood up and said something is not right and has to change. Basically, they fought against the corporate interpretation in which the majority believed, feeling as though they'd found a better way. Unbelievably, this stuff still happens today, which is the obvious reason that there are so many churches out there. This is why your personal devotion time is so critical. You have to give God a chance to speak to you directly in reference to your beliefs and convictions. You have to know what you believe, and the direction you feel God leading you in, and stand on that. When you do this, there will be little room for the beliefs of others to move you.

On the freeway, the speed limit is set at a certain speed, whether it seems fair or unfair. You know what happens when you make the conscious decision to exceed that speed limit. If caught, you are pulled over and given a reality check called a ticket—and then you go on your merry way. However you choose to take care of your ticket, the law does not change. So it is with the body of Christ. No matter the church or the denomination you join, there are rules, politics, and protocols that you must follow. While riding down that lane, if you see that something is not working, then you have a choice to make. That is your pulling-over experience. Your communication with God is your ticket, and then you have to proceed as you see fit, but as mentioned, the law does not change. This is where time and season come in. As much as I have loved some of the places that I have been in Christianity, I had to leave for various reasons. I knew that the location had served its purpose in my life; I got my ticket, and it was time for me to exit from that freeway and detour to another location. No hard feelings; I knew what God had in store for me to do.

PERSUASION

Persuasion is defined by dictionary.com as a deep conviction or belief. This comes when people are not firm in their beliefs or are unlearned or maybe even unsure; such is the case with new believers. When new converts come, there are two types of people drawn to them—those who are there to help and those who think they can help. How do you know the difference? I am glad you asked. Motive! Now, I am not saying to be paranoid and think that everyone is out to get you—God knows that is not the case. But as with everything else in life, you have to be equipped to confront issues that seem to be unclear or that don't agree with your personal convictions and beliefs.

How do you know when to believe? The only way that you should be persuaded is when the objective is based on biblical principles and after you have prayed about the matter and the Holy Ghost leads you a different way. No matter what the denomination is, you know that you are on the right track when they refer to the birth, life, death, burial, and resurrection of Christ. Anything other than those truths should provoke you to run for your life, literally!

When you have a personal relationship with Christ, people can't say much to pull you away from what you know as the truth. This is another type of conviction. When you know the right thing to do but still seem to be pulled away by your own lust or desires, there is a sense of unrest that comes with that decision—until you find your way back to the right place in God.

PURPOSE

Purpose is defined by dictionary.com as the reasons for which something exists or is done, made, or used. Remember that your purpose is your own. You cannot expect everyone to cheer you on from the sidelines. I won't say that this will never happen, but more often than not, it doesn't happen. The reasons behind this are numerous, but just for the record, some of them are ignorance and jealousy, not to mention intimidation. Whenever I find myself in an uncomfortable position in whatever arena I am in, whether it's the workplace, the church, or just in relationships in general, I often ask others in conversation, "Why do you think that …?" Most of the time I get this response: "They are probably just intimidated." This saying used to get under my skin. I never understood what about me could possibly be intimidating. I'm just me. Then one day in my personal devotion after a bitter divorce, I asked God what was wrong with me and why people kept treating me this way. *Why can't I just be normal?* I wondered. I kept hearing God say, "Because you are convicted by your purpose." Don't get me wrong—there have been several times in my life when I just wanted to take the easy road out because it proved to be less hassle and grief, but my conviction in my purpose would not let me do so. There have been churches that turned me away because I am a female preacher, because I was once a lesbian, and for other reasons that I have yet to understand. Although it hurt when that happened, I had to continue to walk in my purpose. Friends of God, I want to share this with you:

Don't expect everyone to celebrate in your parade.
When you find *your* conviction and *your* purpose,
walk in it *no matter the cost.*

Israel Houghton sings a song called "I know who I am." It is so simple in its message: "I am yours and you are mine … Jesus you are mine." Simple in the message but powerful in its purpose.

CHAPTER FOUR:
POLITICS, PERSUASION, AND PURPOSE

Note: It is necessary to be more detailed in your writing in this reflection because you should know why you chose the environment that you worship in, as well as the background behind it. You are empowered by the reflection of your choice of your place of worship and understanding why you made the choice you did.

What denomination do you prefer? _____

Why do you think that is? (If you prefer nondenominational, still explain.)

_____
_____
_____
_____
_____
_____
_____
_____
_____
_____
_____
_____
_____

Look into some of the history of how that denomination came about. (Jot down some key points that are of interest to you.)

_____
_____
_____
_____
_____

_____

_____

_____

_____

_____

_____

What are some areas that you disagree with in that denomination?

_____

_____

_____

_____

_____

_____

_____

_____

_____

_____

_____

How do you think that your purpose can be fulfilled within that denomination?

_____

_____

_____

_____

_____

_____

_____

_____

_____

_____

_____

Will You Dare to Tell Your Story, that someone else will be helped along the way?

CHURCH BODY, CHURCH BUILDING?

When I am preaching, I am often guilty of overusing this sentence: "Can I just be real?" In my subconscious, this often means that I am about to reveal a truth about myself that I know will cause others to judge me. I am still, after all this time, learning to overcome the opinions of man. If God gives us something to say or to share, how dare we ask the permission of the people to say it? It is like when I was a child and I had to say the dreaded Easter speech in front of the church in my big Easter dress and hair bows. After I had worked hard for weeks to remember that speech, I got up to say it and started by asking the permission of the congregation to do so. It just doesn't make sense. It is your assignment to tell your story at the time God tells you to share it. The church body needs you and your story.

Look at this concept:

THE CHURCH BODY

*From whom the whole body **fitly joined together** and compacted by that which every joint supplieth, according to the effectual working in the measure of every part, maketh increase of the body unto the edifying of itself in love.*

—*Ephesians 4:16*

The revelation of this truth is that we are called to be a part of something bigger than we are. When we find our part in the body, which is our purpose, we are irreplaceable in that area. No one can do it like you can. Whatever your gift is, or whatever area in which you are anointed and appointed by God, no one can be you in that capacity. For instance, there may be many singers in your church, but there is only one you, and only you sing your song or do your dance the way that you do. We all have a contribution to make to the body, which is uniquely for us and us alone. There may be people I speak to that I can never move, but then when *you* come into the room and speak into their lives, they are instantly changed. This is what it means to be a part of the church body.

Understanding this truth allows you to maintain your individuality while joining with the body of Christ. This means that you don't have to try to be the next Reverend So-and-So, but you can be who God called you to be, and that is the person who is fearfully and wonderfully made by him. We see in churches all over the world the person who has been the most influential in people's lives. For example, there are many bald-headed men walking around with goatees and suits, speaking in deep and powerful voices. You can look at some of them and see T. D. Jake's influence on their lives. Not that there is anything wrong with having someone in the faith to look up to and maybe even model after, especially when he is working out for the masses; however, we are not designed to lose who we are, to try to be someone else. Be who God called you to be and remain true to your individuality.

There are some body parts that try to operate as another part, which brings about division and can become cancerous in the body of Christ. This will often force the act of an amputation, leaving a negative impact on the body of Christ. What does this mean? I'm glad you asked! For instance, the Bible tells of the different gifts and ministries that should be present in every ministry. For example, perhaps a person is called to be an usher, but as she goes along in the ministry, she feels that she can be a better church secretary. Instead of going and assisting the church secretary who has been appointed for that house, she tries to take over her job. While committing this offense, she soon finds her feelings hurt when she is chastised by the man or woman of God. She winds up leaving the church for the wrong reasons. Now there is a void in the body where that part is supposed to be, and now the entire body suffers because one person was trying to get out of her lane and ride in someone else's. This is what I mean by the amputation of the body part due to the cancerous discord that takes place.

THE CHURCH BUILDING

And it came to pass, as they departed from him, Peter said unto Jesus, Master, it is good for us to be here: and let us make three tabernacles; one for thee, and one for Moses, and one for Elias: not knowing what he said.

—Luke 9:33

Revelation of This Truth

In the days of mega-churches popping up like popcorn all over the land, we have to understand that our work is not so much inside the building. The church is simply where we come to get refueled and celebrate our personal relationship with Christ in a corporate manner. The church building is a common place where we come together to worship and praise our God corporately.

When Peter made the suggestion of the three tabernacles, no one really acknowledged what he said. Jesus was all about his purpose and passion, and he knew that he was just passing through, so an edifice was the least of his worries. In fact, when you read the Bible, you will see that very few miracles took place in the church; most of them were outside of church and among the common man. He and his disciples traveled in packs for the most part, and even while he was pouring into the lives of the people of the outside world, he was investing in the lives of his disciples as well. This is the heart of a true pastor.

Not forsaking the assembling of ourselves together, as the manner of some is; but exhorting one another: and so much the more, as ye see the day approaching.

—*Hebrews 10:25*

We come together to celebrate the ways in which God has drawn us closer to him than we were the day before. We come to church in hopes that our lifestyles outside of the church have compelled someone to come and see the manifestation of the spirit that forces us all to change—and hopefully make that person want to do the same. This is where the appearance of the church building comes into play. Not that I have anything against the mega-churches, but I do have a problem with the minor churches trying to build a mega-church with minor church members, for then they can never help individuals with their deliverance because they are so busy preaching about the offering so that they can make ends meet. That makes the experience lose its savor because that is confirming to the world what they already think (that the church only wants their money), and they walk away feeling the same as when they came. Now, I have seen some ministries that are small but operate in the spirit of excellence until God moves them to the mega-facility, and while they get one that is large enough to accommodate the activities of the church, the upkeep is enough to maintain within their budgets. To me, that is *following the calling, not the crowd.*

Corporate worship can also be a source of individual casualties and even some fatalities. The more that you deal with people, even Christians, the more likely you are to experience a hurt that is more painful than any secular experience that you have ever experienced, and that is mainly because you don't expect to be hurt by church people— but just remember that sometimes the "church building" people lacks the "church body" revelation. I used to be ultimately hurt when things went crazy in the church building, but when I evaluated my life, I realized that because church is where I spend all my time, where else would I get hurt if not in the church? But because God makes it better in that same place, I don't become bitter—I become better.

The correct way to handle an issue (if it comes down to disconnecting yourself) is to leave the church building and go down the street or maybe to the next city and find another church that meets your needs. Understand that I am not saying to be a church hopper, making a habit of going from one church to another. I am saying that if you are attending a church that is contrary to your personal revelation of what the word of God says, then it is best that you disconnect from that particular church and find one that matches your revelation and your personal needs.

Many people frown on people who leave one place and go to another, but I view churches like relationships. Most of us had friends who we crawled around with when we were babies, and though they were important to us at that time, we don't even know their names anymore. Then we went to school and had friends that were our friends this week but not the next week, and the next week we were friends again … yet we may not remember their names either. It is when we became teens that we began to have relationships where we are just beginning to truly learn the names of individuals, and even some of them we don't remember until we pull out our yearbooks. Then there are our adulthood friends who we hardly ever forget because they each affect our lives in a different way. So it is with the church. You church in phases for the most part. By that, I mean that there were churches that I attended as a child because I had no choice, but they laid a foundation for my current relationship with Christ. Then I attended churches that helped form my relationships with people. Ultimately, I want to attend churches that accommodate my current relationship with Christ.

CHAPTER FIVE:
CHURCH BODY, CHURCH BUILDING?

Ask yourself these questions concerning where you are right now in your walk with Christ:

Am I a part of the church body or the church building?

_____

_____

_____

_____

_____

_____

_____

_____

_____

_____

_____

_____

_____

_____

Where in the church body do I fit in?

_____

_____

_____

_____

_____

_____

_____

_____

_____

_____

_____

_____

_____

_____

What are the things that I do well that I can contribute to the body of
Christ? Are there people in the church already doing those things? If
so, how can I assist them?

_____

_____

_____

_____

_____

_____

_____

_____

_____

_____

_____

_____

_____

_____

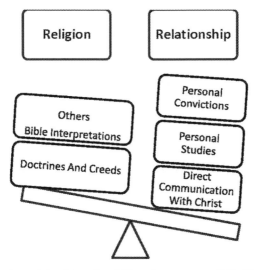

"Balance is critical in the life of a successful Christian"

RELATIONSHIP VERSUS RELIGION

There is a distinct difference between having a *relationship* with Christ and being associated with a religion. The most important foundational truth that I wish one would take away from this book is the need to have a relationship with Christ versus a religious experience without him. I am going to give the first three definitions from the dictionary (per dictionary.com) of each word before I expound on this concept.

Religion is:

1. A set of beliefs concerning the cause, nature, and purpose of the universe, especially when considered as the creation of a superhuman agency or agencies, usually involving

devotional and ritual observances, and often containing a moral code governing the conduct of human affairs.

2. A specific fundamental set of beliefs and practices generally agreed upon by a number of persons or sects.

3. The body of persons adhering to a particular set of beliefs and practices.

Relationship is:

1. A connection, association, or involvement.

2. A connection between persons by blood or marriage.

3. An emotional or other connection between people.

Just in looking at the definitions, you should see where I am going with this. Look at the complexity of the definition of religion and the simplicity of the definition of a relationship. This is key to your walk with Christ.

Relationship will take you where religion can't! When you look at the various sectors of the church, whether Baptist, Apostolic, Protestant, or any other, though they read from the same Bible, you will see that there are spoken and unspoken truths and expectations that come with their denomination, which may not be so clearly present in the word of God. However, they do use the Bible to back up their beliefs. Please understand that anyone can use the Bible to support any cause he or she wants. This was proven in slavery, when the masters used religion or the Bible to persuade the slaves that slavery was right and biblical, when that was far from the truth. This is why having a personal relationship with Christ is so important.

When you have a relationship with Christ instead of the crowd, then you are allowed to grow at a pace that God has designed for you to grow, and he will give you the correct revelation of his word. Even more than that, when transitioning from the world to the church, it is critical that you understand that God *convicts* when the world *condemns*. This critical need to understand this text lies in the fact that when you are involved with some Christians on any level, especially those who may know your past, they have a tendency to not let you forget where you used to be (condemnation). If you're not careful, they will keep you in a place of bondage with their words so you feel as though you will never come out of that place. If you ever find yourself in that place and feel bad, know that this feeling is the convicting power of the Holy Ghost, which is meant to encourage you to get out of the situation that you are in. The painful thing is that when you encounter someone and happen to share your struggle or the fact that you fell, the person may say ignorant things like, "I knew you weren't saved from the beginning!" or "I knew it would happen again; it was just a matter of time!" My friend, ignorance is not bliss!

Per the Bible, "There is therefore now no condemnation for those that are in Christ Jesus" (Romans 8:1, KJV). This single scripture alone lets you know the truth of how God operates. Let's take a minute to evaluate this concept. According to dictionary.com, spiritual conviction is to impress with a sense of guilt; however, condemnation is to judge or pronounce to be *unfit* for use or service. The world is not the only one to condemn us, though. We are often our own worst enemy, and we condemn ourselves before the world has an opportunity to even know about it.

There are three steps to successfully moving forward from whatever your weaknesses are. I created this concept and analogy to make it easier for you to understand. The three simple steps that I am speaking of are to admit, repent, and move on (ARM). Simple, right? It's such a simple concept that is so hard to do. Honestly, oftentimes we find ourselves stuck between the steps, inflicting unnecessary pain on ourselves and our situations. The best advice that I can give you in this chapter is to stretch your ARM to God, and he will take care it. ARM stands for:

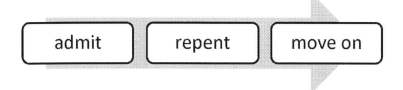

Don't Turn the Knife on Yourself, Give it to God

I remember many of the times when I made a mistake or fell short. I personally felt bad in my spirit, and I didn't really understand what that was. I now know that it was the conviction of the Holy Ghost, which was a direct result of my relationship with him. I knew this because when I prayed and talked to God about it and asked for forgiveness, I felt better. There were also times when either my sin was apparent to the church or I just confessed and it was used against me. I was often forced to relive the guilt of my past sin. There were even times when I myself used my own past to dictate my present and future. This, my friends, is what is called condemnation. This never lets you forget or move past the mistakes that you have made. Condemnation will keep you awake at night, and greater still, it will keep you away from the very destiny that God has created for you. Do not do this to yourself. When you mess up or fall short, honestly and earnestly give it to God and leave it alone. Don't dwell on it because that will make you turn the knife on yourself. It will also make you no good to anyone because no matter how much one may say, "God loves you and so do we," you won't believe it because when you look to heaven, all you see are the mistakes you made on earth.

Remember that God brings conviction, and people (the devil) bring condemnation!

CHAPTER SIX:
RELATIONSHIP VERSUS RELIGION

What am I doing to ensure that I have a relationship, not a religion, with Christ?

_____

_____

_____

_____

_____

_____

_____

_____

_____

_____

_____

_____

_____

_____

_____

_____

_____

_____

_____

_____

_____

_____

_____

_____

_____

_____

_____

_____

_____

Chapter Seven

PROPHESYING VERSUS "PROPHELYING"

Depending on the type or denomination of church you go to, there may be times when people will attempt to speak over your life and tell you that this or that is going to happen. I am not here to persuade you one way or the other about the topic of prophesy. I just want you to be aware of the ways in which the enemy will try to confuse you or turn you away from the very thing that God has in mind for you. I want to equip you with the tool of how to tell the difference between when a person is prophesying and when a person is "prophelying." It goes right back to the foundation of this book, having a personal relationship with Christ. If you have that, it will be difficult for someone to tell you a lie about what God has, will, or is doing in your life. You see, when someone, a prophet, comes into your life and begins to tell you matters about yourself, what is said should not come as a surprise but should be confirmation of something that you and God have already been discussing in your personal prayer time. Seldom is it a newsflash to you. When you receive that word, it should be confirmed in your spirit man about what is going on. I am not saying that there won't be times when God will spring something on you, but more often than not, the prophesy just serves as confirmation to what you already know and feel. Look at this illustration:

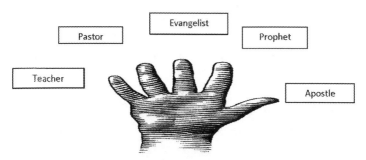

In your Christian walk, you may often hear about the fivefold ministry. This concept is what this diagram depicts. Here is what the explanation is:

Title	Location	Rationale	Role	Scripture
Teacher	Pinky	Feels to be the least but serves as the foundation for ministries	Will be one of the first to interact with new converts to teach them how to convert their minds and hearts to complete conversion	Hebrews 5:12 For when for the time ye ought to be **teachers**, ye have need that one teach you again which be the first principles of the oracles of God; and are become such as have need of milk, and not of strong meat.
Pastor	Ring Finger	Married to the ministry as Christ is to the church	Should show the example of commitment to the body through their commitment to the conversion and clearly shows the transition from change to habit to lifestyle conversion to Christian walk	Jeremiah 3:15 And I will give you **pastor**s according to mine heart, which shall feed you with knowledge and understanding.
Evangelist	The middle finger	Sticks out further than all other fingers on the hand which means that they evangelist is the main one that exemplifies how to go out and bring others in through their gifts which makes room for them	They are the ones to go out and compel men and women to come to the body of Christ and through the example of their lifestyle and relationship with Christ.	2 Timothy 4:5 But watch thou in all things, endure afflictions, do the work of an **evangelist**, make full proof of thy ministry.
Prophet	The pointer finger	Gives direction in the way that God would see fit for the Body to move.	Brings order to the body of Christ through the giving of God-given direction.	Deuteronomy 18:18 I will raise them up a **Prophet** from among their brethren, like unto thee, and will put my words in his mouth; and he shall speak unto them all that I shall command him.
Apostle	The thumb	Is the only part of the hand that is able to touch each and every one of the other fingers.	This means that this individual is able to operate in all of the other roles but touches the lives of the individuals that are serving in each capacity. This is the person whom each individual seeks for guidance in the operation of the individual gifts and callings	1 Corinthians 12:28 And God hath set some in the church, first **apostle**s, secondarily prophets, thirdly teachers, after that miracles, then gifts of healings, helps, governments, diversities of tongues.

Understand that there are several other offices in the church, but these are callings. What is the difference? I'm glad you asked. An office is a position of duty, trust, or authority in the church. A calling means to summon by or as if by divine command. In laymen's terms, an office is where man puts you, but a calling is what God has clearly anointed you to do. For example, the office of a bishop is a biblical office but is not a biblical calling. In essence, every "called apostle" can be a bishop, but not every elected bishop can be an apostle. This is why the attainment of the chapter is so vital. You have to know who you are first before you can accept the responsibility to act as the church expects you to.

CHAPTER SEVEN:
PROPHESYING VERSUS PROPHELYING

In the fivefold ministry, I can see myself and my known attributes leading me to being:

_____

_____

_____

_____

_____

_____

_____

_____

_____

_____

_____

_____

_____

_____

_____

_____

_____

_____

_____

_____

_____

_____

_____

_____

_____

_____

_____

_____

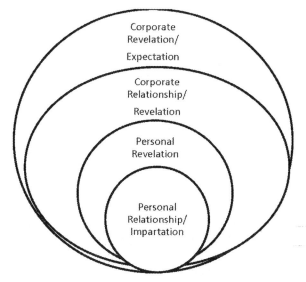

Impartation + Expectation= Revelation

IMPARTATION VERSUS EXPECTATION

Note: This chapter is for the new convert but more so for those of us who are "seasoned Christians" who have a tendency to forget the mission to ensure the success of the new convert.

Churches of today often miss the mark when it comes to the conversion of new believers and assisting in the development of their relationships with Christ. The misconception that often takes place is that when the new converts come, the church focuses on the *expectations* (what the church wants from the individual) and never really focuses on the *impartation* (what the church needs to offer to the individual) that needs to take place to ensure the Christian success of the new convert.

This spiritual neglect leads to a period of frustration and often makes the believer feel as though he or she made a mistake. There are periods or procedures that need to be followed to ensure a balance in the life of every believer.

- Personal relationship/impartation
- Personal revelation
- Corporate relationship/revelation
- Corporate revelation/expectation

The first stage that a believer needs to go through is where impartation is critical to his or her success. It is where his or her personal relationship with Christ is defined through consistent biblical impartation. This means that it is critical for the church to pour into him or her the incomprehensible love of God that sees past all his or her past and current issues, flaws, and shortcomings. This is critical because when we as flesh think of love, we equate it with the love that we experience in the world that is limited to certain criteria. So for one to try to comprehend that someone loves him or her, and that there is absolutely nothing that can be done about it, is impossible to truly understand, no matter how much you read about it or even how much people tell you. As we go through the processes and stages, the prior level or levels don't go away, but they remain as the foundation for growth, and all cycles are ever-growing in the constant exploration of the path to Christendom.

The next stage is where personal revelation takes place. Personal revelation is taking the foundational impartation and beginning to apply it to your personal being. This is also where you begin to make personal connections with Christ as well as establish the validity or application of the impartation that has taken place in your own life. If I had to make a comparison so everyone could clearly understand this concept, I would have to say that this is the adolescent stage of conversion. In natural adolescence, it is the point and place where you seek to find out who you are and where you belong in this world. The same goes for this personal revelation piece of the puzzle. After the impartation that is accompanied with meditation comes revelation, and all of this is still on the personal level.

The third stage is corporate relationship, and revelation is one of the most critical yet vulnerable stages of this process. The reason is because you have spent so much time on yourself and finding out who you are, as well as establishing the ties between you and God, that you have yet to truly partake in the trials and triumphs of commingling with others. The critical part of this is that the two prior processes have to be solidified before this third process can take place. If that doesn't happen, then you will be not only deceived but also manipulated into thinking based on others' perceptions and beliefs. This is where impartation and expectation begin to mesh. There must be a critical balance in this area at this time, and that balance is the responsibility of the individual as well as the overseer under whom he or she serves.

Corporate revelation and expectation is the epitome of this book. This is the place where expectations are somewhat safely placed upon the individual. The key is that the expectations have to be developmentally appropriate for the individual on whom they are placed. Though time has passed, the expectations can still not be too great for the individual to experience some level of success. It's like giving a baby chicken or steak before it has teeth. We have to be wise in our dealings with the vulnerable new birth that has taken place in a person's life, also keeping in mind that all four processes need to continue for the entire life span of the individual. You cannot stop impartation because expectation has begun. In fact, impartation at this point is still critical. It is what we in the education field call the "gradual release of responsibility." This means that you have to follow a process of your own by

- first, showing others how to live this life through your life example;

- second, showing others how to do it by walking them through the correct manner of handling life now that they are converted, according to the Bible in its purest form; and

- third, allowing others to try it on their own with your guidance and help and making sure that they are protected from the judgments of others.

Note to the overseers (seasoned Christians): The overseer has to be sensitive to the Holy Spirit when it comes to the demands that are placed on this individual; you see, this is where the zeal of the new convert can overspeak the balance that is vital to his or her development. Too much responsibility and the person becomes burned out and unreliable; not enough responsibility and he or she becomes lazy and complacent—and maybe even bored enough to go back to the sinful side from which he or she came. This stage in our natural comparison is what we can equate with eighteen- to twenty-one-year-old young adults. They feel as though they can take on the world but have no idea what they are getting themselves into.

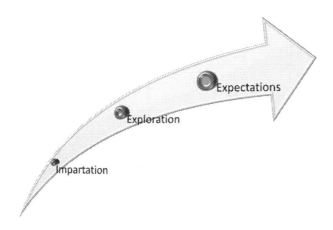

Please understand the spectrum above and know that it has to take place. Note how narrow the end of impartation is in reference to the end of expectations. Though this is the common occurrence that happens in the churches today, it does not mean that is it right; the order is more crucial than anything. You have to partake in serious impartations and then bridge into the exploration to find yourself in the body of Christ, as mentioned in earlier parts of this book. Once you find out who you are and become confident in whose you are, then the process becomes more natural and will balance itself in time.

Simply stated, impartation is the point where you are taught faith and it is birthed in your spirit. The point of exploration is a place wherein your faith is developed, and the point of expectation is the place where your faith is manifested in your words, deeds, and thoughts, which allow you to more freely meet the expectations and demands that may be placed on you by the church. That is what it means to go from faith to faith and glory to glory. A new realm of revelation comes with the development of your faith. Understand that when we are talking about faith, we are talking about faith in God as well as in yourself. The more developed you become in your faith in Christ, the more you begin to walk in the confidence of whose you are—and not so much who you are. This means that a transformation begins to take place wherein you become more dependent on Christ and less dependent on your own abilities.

CHAPTER EIGHT:
IMPARTATION VERSUS EXPECTATION

Five things that I seek to know:

1. _____
   _____
   _____

2. _____
   _____
   _____

3. _____
   _____
   _____

4. _____
   _____
   _____

5. _____
   _____
   _____

Five things that I expect:

1. _____
   _____
   _____

2. _____
   _____
   _____

3. _____
   _____
   _____

4. _____
   _____
   _____

5. _____
   _____
   _____

Five revelations that I have received from this book:

1. _____
   _____
   _____

2. _____
   _____
   _____

3. _____
   _____
   _____

4. _____
   _____
   _____

5. _____
   _____
   _____

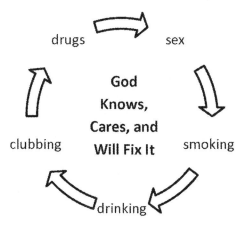

There is no need to be dismayed sin is sin, there is no big or little it's just sin!

NO ONE'S WALK IS THE SAME

Please understand that no two people have the same Christian walk—even if we may have some things in common. This means that my struggles may not be your struggles, and vice versa. Even if we have the same struggles, the level of intensity is completely different from one person to another. For example, consider that drinking is a struggle for two people. One person may struggle with drinking in general and want to stop completely; yet another person may want to decrease from five drinks a day to one drink a day until God completely delivers him or her from the desire. These people would have some of their struggles in common, but they are not the same. One person may be able to overcome his or her stronghold cold turkey after a single experience or encounter with the Lord, which is great, but on the other side of the coin, there are those of us who have to stay in the face of God to find the strength to get through our issues one day at a time.

Many Christians go through certain things in their lives and never share their struggles and how they overcame trials with similarly struggling believers and new converts. The critical need of the church to have real and transparent people is so that we can be a true asset to the church as a body—and not the church as a building. There is a huge difference, and that is one of the foundational truths to this book. Many people who feel as though they are saved because they attend church in a building, and then when they experience anything less than success, the first thing they want to do is leave the church as a body. This means that they have been connected to a church building, and as soon as something makes them angry, then they want to leave the church building and forget the church body. What does this mean? It means they walk away from the church building and quit trying to live right, which affects the church body.

This is not how God designed it to be. A clear and conscious exchange of testimony for the purpose of encouragement and inspiration from one Christian to another is his desire. We are to be helpers to one another. This means that we should be transparent enough for God to be able to share our crosses with one another and not feel judged. Having said that, I have to say that it is not always easy to share our struggles of the past or present with other believers because they are human and judgment is a natural response of the fleshly man. Is it right? No! But it is the truth.

I have been leading praise and worship for many years. I have been singing all of my life, literally, and I have watched the impact that this God-given gift has made on the lives of believers as well as nonbelievers. I remember one Sunday when the Spirit fell so heavily upon me that the very life I wanted to hide, God allowed (though I would say *forced*) me to reveal. It involved my past life of homosexuality, which only a few of my closest friends and family members knew about. When the Spirit of God fell on me and I was compelled to tell just a nugget of my story, I remember seeing the reaction of the people toward me. There were individuals who realized that if I could come through that and still have the power of God evident through my ministry, then surely they could come out of their situations as well because God has no respect of person; he loves us all the same. What he does for one, he can and will do for all—if you want it. It was not easy to talk about that, nor my rape, adulterous spirit, teen pregnancy, and all the sins that had beset me so many times, but I truly thank God for his mercy, and I know that I really can do all things through Christ who strengthens me. This is what ministry is about: helping one another, not hurting one another. Oftentimes we can't even get our deliverance and breakthrough because we won't help someone who needs us.

Judgment comes from ignorance, when people don't understand or have never experienced something. People are apt to judge issues that they have never encountered, and because they are not able to grasp the ins and outs of an issue, they do what I call an "outer experience judgment call," which means that they just speak about a thing from the perspective of ignorance, saying things such as, "If I were you, this is what I would do …" It is not fair to make this type of statement on issues that are critical to another individual.

I have often said that it would be lovely if every church could have a directory of the issues that believers have faced and overcome in their lives so that when new believers came in facing the same issues, they could call the members in the directory, consulting others for advice on how to come out of the situation. The question is, are there people real enough to put their names in the directory or not too proud to use the directory to assist their walk in Christ? More often than not, the answer is no.

If you knew that your story could help someone along the way, would you tell it? Would you put yourself out there and run the risk of judgment from your fellow Christian friends? Would your pride allow you to be who you are and to tell who you were?

CHAPTER NINE:
NO ONE'S WALK IS THE SAME

The assignment for this chapter is to take a moment to reflect upon what you have overcome in your life—and how you think that sharing that obstacle can help someone else in that walk.

What have I seen God already fix in me? (For example, perhaps you don't drink/smoke as much as you used to.)

_____

_____

_____

_____

_____

_____

_____

_____

_____

_____

If I had only one story to tell that I thought would be the most profound in the life of another Christian, what would it be?

_____

_____

_____

_____

_____

_____

_____

_____

_____

_____

_____

_____

_____

_____

_____

_____

_____

_____

_____

_____

_____

_____

_____

_____

_____

_____

_____

When I talk to others, am I truly real about who I am, where I am going, and what I have been through?

_____

_____

_____

_____

_____

_____

_____

_____

_____

_____

_____

_____

_____

_____

_____

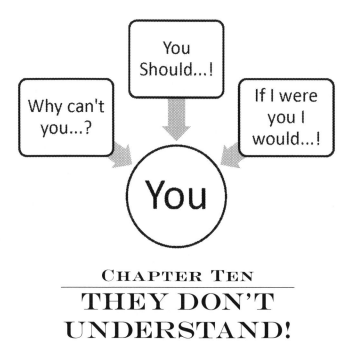

THEY DON'T UNDERSTAND!

One of the greatest mistakes that we make is expecting people to understand or even care where we are coming from. People of God, this just doesn't happen—or I should say that this rarely happens. There have been times when I went through my storms and knew that no one understood, but I would sit back and watch them say that they did because that is what I wanted to hear. The hard part about this truth is that when I realized or they showed me the truth that they really didn't understand, I found myself heartbroken, disappointed, and upset. We cannot expect everyone to accept or understand our struggles. Though others may honestly try and with all good intentions want to, it just may not be in them to do so, and you can't be upset with them for that.

There was a time in my singing career when I found myself heartbroken because I felt as though people knew the voice but not the victim that I thought I was. Even when I got the revelation that I am not the victim but the victor, I still wanted them to get to know the victor as well as the voice. The reason I felt this was important was because the voice was never guaranteed, but the victory that God gave to me was. Though "You see the glory, but you don't know my story" is a cliché, it is one of the most truthful statements attesting to the life that I live. People see the power that my voice brings in presentation, but they don't understand the persecution that I had to go through, and even now still endure, to receive this precious anointing from God. But because I know this truth, I am able to go through with grace because I know it increases the passion in my performances.

We do want people to understand, especially if they have already been where we are, but there are a few things that we have to remember when trying to release this spirit of expectation that we have on people:

- They often don't want to be real about their deliverance due to the fear associated with how the crowd will view them now that they are in their new place in God.

- They have been delivered so long from that thing that they forgot what it was like to be in that bondage, and some honestly don't remember how they got out to help you through the process.

- Rarely, but it does happen, people are so busy in the church body, doing whatever, that they neglect to see the issues that are at hand, and the sad thing is that they write it off as your being weak and ungodly, saying that it's up to you to defend yourself and tell what's really going on in your life. At that point, they are held accountable for the actions that they take in reference to your situation, but no matter what you do, you have to stay focused and remember that your relationship with Christ is what matters most.

I have found these three freedom nuggets fundamental in helping me understand my own walk. Again, I can't say this enough. I am not bashing people but trying to save people from falling into the same pits that I have in days gone by and, honestly, even sometimes still struggle with now. People are people, and I am me. I cannot change people, and people cannot change me—only God can. The reason for this book is to help all to understand how life inside the church works, and though it's a harsh truth from time to time, it is the truth, and the sooner we recognize and rectify it, the better off the body of Christ will be.

To go from faith to faith and glory to glory, a purification process has to take place. This process is ongoing forever and always in the life of a healthy Christian. What is a healthy Christian? One who seeks to grow continually, no matter the cost associated with the process. In this process, there are several cycles repeating simultaneously in your walk. In the background, there is always the ARM theory, wherein you admit, repent, and move on. This is continually happening because what I call the DC³ theory (discovery, confrontation, consolation, and conclusion) is taking place, and that is where there is a continual self-evaluation going on. In that self-evaluation and the DC³ theory, all steps must be followed.

The DC³ Theory in conjunction with the A.R.M. Theory

"Simultaneous action for sanctified deliverance"

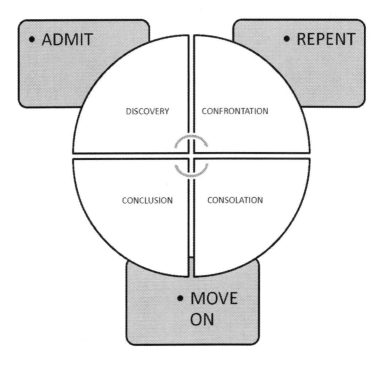

Discovery—This means that I (the Christian) am continually discovering new faults and hidden sins that I have. As I discover them, I have to confront them head-on.

Confrontation—This is one of the most critical but also the most painful parts. You see, every time you confront your old self, you are stripping away part of the inner you that has always been there and always been comfortable.

Consolation—When you begin to strip the "old you" away, it is only natural to feel weak and vulnerable, hence the term "stronghold." A stronghold can be a sin that has made you feel strong and confident in who you are and what you are doing. When that is taken away, then there is naturally a feeling of weakness that steps in and makes you feel vulnerable—and in all actuality, you are. That is why we have to be careful of whom we are around when we are in these conditions. CAUTION: whatever you do, make sure that your consolation in these matters comes from Christ alone.

Note: The reason this is so critical is that in your weakened state, if you find consolation in the wrong thing or person, you are apt to create a new stronghold. For example, when I was being delivered from my first homosexual relationship, I still associated with other lesbians because I thought that I was strong enough. I had discovered the problem, which was my homosexual lifestyle, and I confronted it by getting out of the relationship, but instead of seeking God for consolation, I went to other individuals who had yet to be delivered from their sexual disorientation and found consolation in them, only to find my conclusion to be bisexuality, which created a bigger problem. How did that happen? Because in their consolation, I was made to feel as if it was okay for me to be that way because I was getting the best of both worlds … *Not!* I had to start the cycle all over again, and this time I sought God and only God, guarding my everything until the process was complete. How did I know that the process was complete? When I saw the old girlfriend, there was no attraction, and even her physical appearance looked different. Then when I looked at men, I felt the same way, so I had to ask God what was happening to me, and he told me that my eyes and affections were to be set on him until I was strong enough again to handle sexual attractions to anyone. Ultimately, I believe he was saying that all my energy needed to be saved for my God-sent husband (whom I have yet to discover, so God has given me new loves such as my career and my ministry until the time comes).

We were just talking about the DC³ theory, and we never really discussed the ARM theory that was happening in the background. Remember: admit, repent, and move on. So during this process, as I was going through my transformation, yes, I had thoughts and even acted on them from time to time, but I had to remember the ARM theory so that I could continue in my DC³. This is what I mean when saying these processes are continual and simultaneous—they go hand in hand. It's like your heart is beating and you are breathing at the same time. It just happens, and you never consciously think about it until it's brought to your attention. Many just don't understand that this is happening, but now you can share it with them.

Conclusion: Always be careful to close the chapters in this area. If this issue caused you pain, make sure that you don't relive this pain by consistently talking about it. The more you talk about it and rehearse your pain, the further you are away from deliverance from that thing.

The DC^3 Theory in conjunction with the A.R.M. Theory

"Simultaneous action for sanctified deliverance"

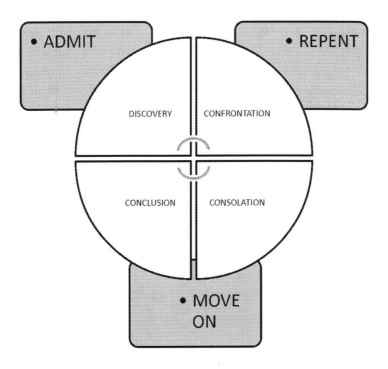

CHAPTER TEN:
THEY DON'T UNDERSTAND!

What are three issues in my life in which I need to make sure I use the DC³ theory (those that I have started but not completed or need to get started on)? For the issues that I have begun working on, what phase of the DC³ theory am I in?

1. _____
_____
_____

2. _____
_____
_____

3. _____
_____
_____

What are five things that I wish that people understood about me?

1. _____
_____
_____

2. _____
_____
_____

3. _____
_____
_____

4. _____
_____
_____

5. _____
_____
_____

What are five things that I wish I understood about people?

1. _____
   _____
   _____

2. _____
   _____
   _____

3. _____
   _____
   _____
   _____

4. _____
   _____
   _____
   _____

5. _____
   _____
   _____

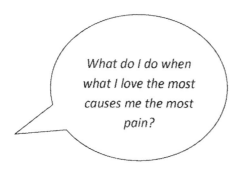

What do I do when
what I love the most
causes me the most
pain?

CHAPTER ELEVEN

THE PAIN OF MY PASSION

I remember someone once prophesying to me, saying, "The thing that I have a passion for is what causes me the most pain." This statement has never left my spirit. I want to transfer this prophesy to you because you must understand and be equipped to realize that the one thing that you love the most is the one thing that the devil will use to bring you the most grief. The method to the madness in this case is that because it is your passion, you will be the greatest threat to the devil's kingdom in that area. The passion that is conveyed in that act will be more profound than the particulars of the action. This means that because I have a passion for singing, the passion that is conveyed in my performances outweighs the particulars, such as notes and timing. I am a worshipper from my heart, and singing praise and worship is my passion. That passion has been the most painful operation that I have participated in at any given church. It hurts me to my heart to see individuals play with my one lifeline that brings me through every situation and circumstance that I have endured throughout my life. To see a person taint the very worship that paints the picture of my pain when I can't put it into words aggravates me, and if it does that to me, I just try to imagine how God feels about it, and that angers me. The devil knows that through the anointing that God has placed over my life in reference to singing,

65

many people are helped and yokes are destroyed simply because of the anointing, not me. Well, if he (the devil) can anger me by allowing me to see the tainted worship of others and he knows that my reaction will be to stop singing, then he knows that he has won because of the fact that since there is no passion *de*picted, then further pain can be *in*flicted on the ones who are lost and gone astray. This is what I mean by the pain of my passion. When you find that one thing that you love to do for God, and you do it well and effectively, you can rest assured that it is the very thing that the devil will use to hurt you. Beware and push past the pain, continuing in your passion.

Tips for Pushing Past Your Pain

- Someone said *push* means "pray until something happens." Another acronym for this could be "pursue until the shift happens," wherein your passion becomes prevalent.

- Stay focused; stay true! Don't let the pain prevail over your passion and make you want to give up, leaving a loophole in the body.

- Purge yourself until the manifestation of the removal of the pain is completed. This may mean separating yourself from people and some of the things that you love the most and entering into a fast so that you can hear directly from God on the matter.

CHAPTER ELEVEN:
THE PAIN OF MY PASSION

What are the three things that I am most passionate about?

1. _____
   _____
   _____

2. _____
   _____
   _____

3. _____
   _____
   _____

Note: Understanding this revelation will help you to know what the devil will likely use against you to inflict pain.

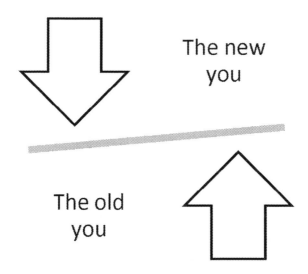

The new you

The old you

"You mean God can use me just the way that I am? YES"

FROM EARTH TO HEAVEN

As we wrap up this reading, it is my prayer that you have been enlightened by what you have read. The epitomized truth to this story is that you can be you and only you. There are certain attributes and characteristics in you that God designed that way, and they won't change—but the motive behind them will. Certain characteristics have remained consistent over the course of my life, and when I was saved, God didn't change them about me; however, he changed the way I handled them. I encourage you to do some self-evaluation in these pages and see what attributes you have always had, and how God can, is, or will use them to the advantage of the kingdom. Look at what I mean:

In the world	Me	For God
Use to fight people at the drop of the dime never thinking about the other person	violent	Now I fight the devil in the spiritual realm and fight for others as well
Used to laugh at people and use them as comedic material to make a dime or just to mask the pain of my life	funny	Now I make people laugh by pointing out my own personal flaws but I am sure to show them how God turned or is turning it around. This also assists in bringing comfort to them in reference to becoming a part of the body of Christ.
Wasn't always this characteristic as a matter of fact for many years I struggled with self esteem issues but when I got the revelation of whose I am the confidence came with the package	confident	Used as a tool to encourage others to know in whom their trust should lie and what to do with it in the meantime. There is a difference between confidence and arrogance which is discussed in this chapter so keep reading
When I was in the world I was passionate about whatever I did. I was what some called a chief sinner, if I was going to do it, I went all out and got it done and made sure all t's were crossed and I's dotted	passionate	When I got saved God never took my passion away but now I am a chief worshipper if there is such a thing, I still have the same zeal and commitment but now it's for God.
I have never been one to have a problem telling people how I feel even if it meant creating a word. Yes, I was one of those neck rolling, finger snapping, eyes rolling; don't make me take my earrings off type people.	articulate	I now use my vocabulary to try and encourage the body of Christ and to compel men and women to come to Christ. Now don't get me wrong I still create a word here and there but not to harm but to help.
I was not always a big one for fashion because I felt other things were important and comfort was above all other things, but when I started to dress I really started dressing, wearing whatever showed the most and whatever drew the most attention.	Fashionable	When I turned my life over my fashion sense changed. I love clothes because I think that it is important that people see that you can be saved and be sexy in a Godly kind of way. You can be fully covered and still draw attention because sexiness is an attitude of confidence and stability but still leaves a lot to the imagination that is to be discovered only with time and energy.
I used to always drop my head when someone paid me a compliment. Many times it was because I felt as though they were lying to me or just saying that to get something in return.	modest	I now know how to graciously accept a compliment from time to time and view it as an opportunity to tell others that God is no respect of person and can do the same for you. This way I take none of God's glory because it all belongs to him and that's for real
I have always been smart. I remember I used to be one to read the dictionary for fun because I wanted to be smarter than everyone else and I wouldn't share the knowledge because then I wouldn't be the smartest and I wanted to keep one leg up on everyone else.	scholarly	I am big on research and knowledge because without it we are quick to be deceived but now I am eager to share the knowledge to empower others as well.

Realize that you may be the very balance that the body of Christ needs. You can show your worldly friends and the church folk as well that you can be cool and saved. I find that in many cases, people are attracted to my humor first, and though at times it used to aggravate me because oftentimes I wasn't even trying to be funny, I found that comedy is a hidden gift that makes students more attentive in my teaching, more relaxed in my preaching, and more intrigued in my other efforts. You see, what churches lack nowadays are the elements of fun. We make people feel as though they have to drop the fun and look like a nun. This is so far from the truth. We as Christians ought to be the most beautiful creatures inside and out, just because of whom we serve. It's not arrogant or conceited for one to acknowledge her or his own assets and beauty. It is echoing the feelings of God in Genesis when he looked at what he made and said, "It was good!" You have got to be able to look at what God made you into, even in its incomplete state, and say, "I am good because he made me!" Never mind what others say.

I share my stories in this book to show the change that God has created in me and the impact that his presence has had in my life. Sure, there will be those who will view this book in their own way or see it as a sense of arrogance leaping off the page. Arrogance is defined as offensive display of superiority or self-importance; overbearing pride. Confidence is defined by dictionary.com as "full trust; belief in the powers, trustworthiness, or reliability of a person or thing." For many years, I felt inferior, but when I allowed Christ into my life for real and began to build my knowledge base, I realized that knowledge truly is power, cliché notwithstanding. My self-esteem began to rise as the Christ within me rose, and now I walk as a Philippians 1:6 woman: "Being confident of this very thing, that he which hath begun a good work in you (me) will perform it until the day of Jesus Christ ..." This means that no matter how many CDs I record or how many books I sell, I stand confident not in who I am but in *whose* I am. I understand that it's not about me but all about thee and what he has done in my life. People of God, be blessed, be happy, and be prosperous, knowing that churchin' has just became easier!

CHAPTER TWELVE:
FROM EARTH TO HEAVEN

How will you implement balance in your life as a Christian?

_____

_____

_____

_____

_____

_____

_____

_____

_____

_____

_____

_____

_____

_____

_____

Complete this chart about yourself and see how you think God can use your attributes to his glory.

In the World	Me	For God

POINTS FOR SELF-EVALUATION

The reason for the duplication of these questions in this book is to serve as a resource for later use or as a point of quick reference when sharing the contents with your loved ones.

WELCOME

What are some things that I desire for God to change in me? _____

_____

_____

_____

_____

_____

_____

_____

_____

_____

_____

_____

_____

_____

_____

_____

_____

_____

_____

WHAT AM I SUPPOSED TO DO NOW?

What are five questions that I wish someone would answer?

1. _____
   _____
   _____

2. _____
   _____
   _____

3. _____
   _____
   _____

4. _____
   _____
   _____

5. _____
   _____
   _____

WHY SO MANY?

Go visit five churches and then compare them in reference to likes and dislikes. Then rank the objectives below from one to five, with one being complete dislike and five being the one liked most.

Preaching	1	2	3	4	5
Teaching	1	2	3	4	5
Singing	1	2	3	4	5
Development	1	2	3	4	5
Discipline	1	2	3	4	5

POLITICS, PERSUASION, AND PURPOSE

What denomination do you prefer? _____

Why do you think that is? (If you prefer nondenominational, still explain.)

_____

_____

_____

_____

_____

_____

_____

_____

_____

_____

_____

_____

_____

_____

Look into some of the history of how that denomination came about. (Jot down some key points that are of interest to you.)

_____

_____

_____

_____

_____

_____

_____

_____

_____

_____

_____

_____

_____

What are some areas that you disagree with in that denomination?

_____

_____

_____

_____

_____

_____

_____

_____

_____

_____

_____

_____

_____

_____

_____

How do you think that your purpose can be fulfilled within that denomination?

_____

_____

_____

_____

_____

_____

_____

_____

_____

_____

_____

_____

_____

_____

CHURCH BODY, CHURCH BUILDING?

Ask yourself these questions concerning where you are right now in your walk with Christ:

Am I a part of the church body or the church building?

_____
_____
_____
_____
_____
_____
_____
_____
_____
_____
_____
_____
_____
_____
_____
_____
_____

Where in the church body do I fit in?

_____
_____
_____
_____
_____
_____
_____
_____
_____
_____
_____

What are the things that I do well that I can contribute to the body of Christ? Are there people in the church already doing those things? If so, how can I assist them?

_____

_____

_____

_____

_____

_____

_____

_____

_____

_____

_____

_____

_____

_____

_____

_____

_____

_____

_____

_____

_____

_____

_____

_____

_____

_____

_____

_____

_____

CAN YOU STAND TO BE REAL?

If I had only one story to tell that I thought would be the most profound in the life of another Christian, what would it be?

When I talk to others, am I real about who I am, where I am going, and what I have been through?_____

_____

_____

_____

_____

_____

_____

_____

_____

_____

_____

_____

_____

_____

_____

_____

_____

_____

_____

_____

_____

_____

_____

_____

_____

_____

_____

_____

_____

_____

_____

_____

RELATIONSHIP VERSUS RELIGION

What am I doing to ensure that I have a relationship, not a religion, with Christ?

PROPHESYING VERSUS PROPHELYING

In the fivefold ministry, I can see myself and my known attributes leading me to being:

_____

_____

_____

_____

_____

_____

_____

_____

_____

_____

_____

_____

_____

_____

_____

_____

_____

_____

_____

_____

_____

_____

_____

_____

_____

_____

_____

_____

_____

_____

_____

_____

_____

_____

_____

_____

_____

IMPARTATION VERSUS EXPECTATION

Five things that I seek to know:

1. _____
_____
_____
_____

2. _____
_____
_____

3. _____
_____
_____

4. _____
_____
_____

5. _____
_____
_____

Five things that I expect:

1. _____
_____
_____

2. _____
_____
_____

3. _____
_____
_____

4. _____
_____
_____

5. _____
_____
_____

Five revelations that I have received from this book:

1. _____
_____
_____

2. _____
_____
_____

3. _____
_____
_____

4. _____
_____
_____

5. _____
_____
_____

NO ONE'S WALK IS THE SAME

What have I seen God already fix in me?

_____
_____
_____
_____
_____

THEY DON'T UNDERSTAND!

What are three issues in my life in which I need to make sure I use the DC^3 theory (those that I have started but not completed or need to get started on)? For the issues that I have begun working on, what phase of the DC^3 theory am I in?

1. _____
   _____
   _____

2. _____
   _____
   _____

3. _____
   _____
   _____

What are five things that I wish that people understood about me?

1. _____
   _____
   _____

2. _____
   _____
   _____

3. _____
   _____
   _____

4. _____
   _____
   _____

5. _____
   _____
   _____

What are five things that I wish I understood about people?

1. _____
   _____
   _____

2. _____
   _____
   _____

3. _____
   _____
   _____

4. _____
   _____
   _____

5. _____
   _____
   _____

FROM EARTH TO HEAVEN

How will you implement balance in your life as a Christian?

_____

_____

_____

_____

_____

_____

_____

_____

_____

Complete this chart about yourself and see how you think God can use your attributes to his glory.

In the World	Me	For God

For bookings or more information, please feel free to visit my website at jgilbertministries.com. All of my contact information is there. I would love to hear from you and answer any questions that you may have. Be blessed!

EPILOGUE

As the author, this book has been therapeutic for me, and I hope that in some way, it makes your walk easier in your relationship with Christ as well as with the church body. The trials and tribulations that I went through during the production of this project served as the reassurance that I needed that the body needs this kind of self-help that the world speaks of when it comes to Christendom. Be blessed, my brothers and sisters, and know that I would love to hear from you and how this book has blessed your life.